More Than One Way Home

by Jeffrey L. Baxter

DORRANCE
PUBLISHING CO
EST. 1920
PITTSBURGH, PENNSYLVANIA 15238

Dorrance Publishing Co
585 Alpha Drive
Suite 103
Pittsburgh, PA 15238
Visit our website at *www.dorrancebookstore.com*

ISBN: 978-1-4809-5000-9
eISBN: 978-1-4809-4977-5

More Than
One Way Home

There's more than one way home
Ain't no right way, ain't no wrong
And whatever road you might be on
You find your own way
'Cause there's more than one way home.

Keb Mo
"More Than One Way Home"

Foreword

I had intended to retire from teaching high school English in 2010 when my youngest child, Olivia, graduated from the University of Missouri. I weighed 460 pounds and my knees ached so much from bearing the onerous cargo of my body that I could not walk more than several hundred steps a day. That I was still teaching was itself a miracle. I had suffered depression through much of the nineties and genuinely pondered whether my life was worth living. This book is about how I recovered from chronic depression, lost more than two hundred pounds, and redeemed my teaching career, and, more importantly, my life. I am the 2014 Kansas Teacher of the Year.

My wife, Connie, was the first to realize that I needed help. Friend, companion, lover, and my best part, her blessings made me a better person than I deserved to be. Next, a caring therapist helped reconnect me to my true self, deal with the oppressive issues I'd borne for nearly twenty years, and rediscover my Grandma Younkin's life lessons—the core of who I am. This therapeutic process of reconnecting to childhood memories ultimately uncovered the dark seeds of my depression.

The concept for the book originated from writing assignments I did with my students as they reflected on their own youthful experiences: "Neighborhood Map," "This I Believe," "Dear Fifteen-Year-Old Me," and "Resume Virtues vs. Eulogy Virtues" were some of the prompts that evoked the most remarkable narratives. The Greater Kansas City Writing Project, under the kindhearted leadership of Katie Kline, helped me discover my voice and find my style in telling these stories. Ted Fabiano read drafts of the stories and made astute suggestions that helped me to "show, not tell." Dylan Carter, LuAnn Fox, and Scot Squires were invaluable critics. Teaching partner and poet Al Ortulani helped me fine-tune my diction. Brad LeDuc, innovative artist and teacher, designed the book's cover. Most importantly, these are all treasured friends.

As my stories were shared, students, teachers, parents and family members insisted that I assemble the stories into a book. Along the way, I came up with the idea of introducing the childhood memory chapters with recollections of the therapy sessions that spawned them. I've learned that memories are never replications of exactly what happened. Memories are either better or worse than the actual events. Nevertheless, they are true.

I believe this is a memoir that will inspire the anxious, the depressed, and the confused—anyone. I know my students will enjoy learning why I am who I am. Healing begins with the commitment to that first step and understanding that you cannot do this alone. Everyone needs a Grandma Younkin. *More Than One Way Home* is about the restoration of hope.

Prologue

In Great Bend, Kansas, cool spring winds breathe life into the yellowed wheat growing incrementally toward June harvest. The fresh smell of newly plowed earth blends with the stirring of chickens, cows, horses, and hogs awakened by the dog's yelp and the slapping of farmhouse screen doors. Farmers hitch the last buckle on their stained overalls as they tread resolutely toward red-scarred barn doors to begin the five o'clock feedings. At that moment, the life cycle of western Kansas slowly rises against the backdrop of a breathtaking sunrise stretched seamlessly across the flat horizon—timeless and eternal.

Great Bend sits at the apex of an inverted "U" of the Arkansas (pronounced R-Kansas) River—hence, Great Bend. From the outskirts of town, one can easily imagine Cheyenne Indian scouts—faces painted for war—scanning the rugged skyline searching for the dusty trail smoke of the 7th Cavalry. From that same vantage point today, one can see sandhill cranes, yellowthroat warblers, and scores of endangered species returning as they do annually to the 41,000 acres of the Cheyenne Bottoms Wildlife Refuge, named for those same Cheyenne Indians.

Great Bend residents—rural and town—know the rhythms of nature that make *God's country* unique: the undulating whisper of the Arkansas River as it ruffles against the sandy banks under the US-281 bridge, and the mix of sour corrosive oil and shredded flanged fittings that sludge roadways leading to oil derricks. Simultaneously, lines of scooters, bikes, and stick shift cars congest Morton Street before the beginning of every work and school day. In unison, the smells and sounds portend the start of another day—a sacred ritual in western Kansas forgotten in the teeming city life of Kansas City and Wichita.

Great Benders of the early 60s weren't that much different from the Barton County homesteaders of more than a hundred years before. Each family member did his job, ate dinner around the kitchen table at 5:30, worshipped together on Sundays, and laughed and sighed at births and deaths as the occasion called for.

With my parents, one brother, and two sisters, I grew up in a small three-bedroom brick house at 2305 Franklin Street where Mom and Dad, the embodiment of June and Ward Cleaver, tucked us in each night under quilts pieced by Grandma's ladies' circle.

I remember how Randy Yowell, Jon Briel, Terry Claasen, and I connived countless ways to make mischief on the nuns at St. Rose—more than God should have allowed. But for Grandma's incessant evening prayers, we would have been cast into hellfire for sure.

In 1960, Roosevelt Junior High served mostly the children raised by blue collars—factory workers, oil riggers, shoe salesmen, clerks, cashiers, nurses, secretaries, and postal workers. My Dad was a postman, and so I went to Roosevelt. The bankers, lawyers, and doctors lived in the wealthier west part of town and went to the more fashionable Harrison Junior High. That the students of the two junior highs would meld at the high school level was always a dramatic issue.

While Harrison students celebrated their affluence with better cafeteria food, shinier hallways, cooler uniforms, and cuter girls, Roosevelt students worried about getting through the gauntlet of Moonlight Raiders, a local street gang that routinely tore the hell out of City Park and intimidated teachers and students just by the sheen of their black leather jackets with the white crescent moons inked on the back. Oily duck-tailed hairdos, ankle high dungarees, and pearl-handled switchblades completed their uniforms and told the timid to step lightly. Metal detectors in schools were thirty years away, so these bullies became a compulsory right-of-passage to matriculate from Roosevelt to Great Bend High School. The high school mascot was the Black Panther, a name that sounded inimitable and fierce. From the perspective of the '70s, the irony of that mascot as a symbol of racial protest was not lost on anyone.

Ethnically, Great Bend was mostly German, Dutch, and Welsh immigrants—generations of hard-working, farm-loving white folk, aware of their

African-American and Hispanic neighbors, but not quite willing to call them fellow citizens yet. That changed for me during the summer of my first year of high school when I got a job packing hides for Thies Beef Packing Company on Saturday mornings.

This sweat-soaked, back-breaker of a job required a crew of twelve to shake the cow hides free of the salt preservative, fold them in quarters, bind them with twine, and deposit them on a conveyer belt that trundled upward to a waiting diesel semi-truck. There were twelve workers: seven Blacks, four Hispanics, and me. That we were paid in cash through a jail-barred window oddly made the job seem even more chic. I kept this job for the rest of high school, and it was a formative basis of my physical development, not to mention an introduction to racial understanding, that has stood me in good stead for more than fifty years. Working as equals, coordinating our efforts with equanimity, this crew of twelve became my brethren long before the Civil Rights Act became law.

My tranquil childhood, racial bonding, and the growing tumult of the '60s collided at the intersection of November 22, 1963, when President John Kennedy was assassinated. The voiceless high school hallways and the muted basketball practice at day's end stood in stark contrast to a normal Friday—only the thunks of dribbling and smacking of balls off backboards broke the silence. That event became the fulcrum of my high school education, and things were never the same: left distanced from right, Black alienated from non-Black, and journalism malformed from reporting to sensationalizing to polarizing. The flood of emotions burned as the flag-draped coffin was saluted by the dead president's young son.

I grew up on the brink of Vietnam War protests, James Taylor's contemplative folk songs, four political assassinations, Woodstock, and Watergate. But, most of all I remember my parents, brother, sisters and friends who made going through the tumult bearable, even life-affirming.

And, always, Grandma.

My healing would take me back to these days for refuge and revelation. I didn't know then how consequential the memories would be for my salvation. Redemption never comes easily and always has stories to tell.

August 1998

The black hole loomed deeper than the night before. Spinning counter-clockwise this time, gyrating unevenly, it sucked the gray image of me downward into a dark vortex. The soundless screams working mechanically from my mouth went unheeded, while the throbbing of a tedious heartbeat tolled tonelessly, discordantly. It would be a long night. I had survived many.

Mel noted during our sessions that the black hole seemed to come at any time, day or night, at the behest of a variety of triggers. A telephone's ring, a knock on the door, a passerby's greeting—but mostly it was Damien's voice. Stern, cold, unforgiving, his voice triggered the scaffolding terror that paralyzed and plunged me into the dark hole quickly.

Mel's image, on the other hand, spoke kindness, even hope. Short, bespectacled, and with a thin, receding hairline, he dressed frumpily in khakis, button-down shirt, and sweater vest. His clothes always seemed two sizes too large, and his belt made his pants gather in places unintended. His eyes smiled, and his carpentry-worn hands and relaxed touch were grandfatherly. I had never met a more genial man.

I told him that I had never known the hole's end, was never rescued from it. Each nightmare ended with me washing ashore on the banks of the hole's coil like driftwood lurching to a stop on a riverbank. I would awaken sobbing, sniveling with damp, teary rivulets and rims of grayness lapping beneath my eyes. A world without end, almost hopeless. Almost.

Mel and I had met weekly in his office since July of 1996. At each meeting, we peeled back the layers of the onion, trying to discover how to prevent the triggers from their terrible work; how to silence Damien's voice. These sessions were the only times I felt safe. Talking about the black hole was oddly uplifting, as if discussing it rendered it harmless, clinically examining it like a corpse on a gurney. And so I looked forward to our sessions as a safe harbor from the black hole's ebbing pull.

But each session, sooner or later, was followed by darkness. My hyperactive mind could snag a streaking memory from the speeding synapses and spark the blackness without a real event. My heart would pulsate like I was running from demons, and the plunge would begin.

Week after week, this Sisyphean drama continued. One day, Mel asked me to recall the one time in my life when I felt safest, most secure, and at peace. The image came slowly, smoothly like a conical stage light rising on a scene from my childhood: Grandma Younkin and me on those paint-chipped, green rocking chairs on the front porch at 1301 Morton in Great Bend, Kansas.

Creak-uch, creak-uch, creak-uch.

1948 – 1956

I was born in an ambulance on the corner of Linwood and Gilham in Kansas City in the winter of 1948. The medical personnel, monitoring my mother's wheezing and erratic breathing, were stunned when intense contractions unexpectedly commenced within a quarter mile of Mercy Hospital. With one EMT comforting my mother, another navigated the premature baby through the gush of amniotic fluid, while the driver caromed expertly through the downtown traffic.

I was the firstborn child to Hiram and Patricia Baxter. Hi was a farmer who enlisted as a Marine medic shortly after Pearl Harbor. Pat was the youngest of five—Pishy-Patty-Poo, to her three older brothers. She worked at the American State Bank in Great Bend. After the war, they met and fell in love, married, and moved to Kansas City in their 1944 Chevy Fleet Master so Hi could study architecture.

And then calamity intervened.

Pat became pregnant with me and was shortly thereafter diagnosed with tuberculosis. The race began to see which would culminate first—her hospitalization or my birth. On January 21, Hi and Pat were in the ambulance together and about to find out.

My name—Jeffrey Lynn—was chosen because it passed Grandma Younkin's yelling-out-the-back-door test, a time-honored Younkin tradition which determined how readily a name could be barked to beckon children home. Grandma was nothing if not practical, principled, and perspicacious—apparently the perfect qualities for taking care of a grandson.

As was the custom of the time, I was quarantined from my mother because of her tuberculosis. Our bonding was restricted to observations through a smudgy window. Like lepers, tuberculins were isolated, and doctors didn't know what to do with TB-offspring. So Grandma Younkin, at the age of sixty-six, a retired English teacher, took on the charge of nurturing me. No one knew at the time how meaningful that would be.

Since my parents' medical insurance didn't cover tuberculosis, Hi gave up his architectural study in order to work full-time to pay the large hospital bill. My parents were left penniless, but owed no one. And so we all moved back to Grandma's for a fresh start.

Great Bend, Kansas, was a bustling town on the oil routes to Wichita in the 1950s. Grandma Younkin's house at 1301 Morton was three blocks away from the busiest street, but it might as well have been a hundred miles. The most prominent feature of the house was the spacious front porch. On it sat two faded-green rocking chairs with rainbow-colored burlap cushions. Grandma would rock like a metronome greeting each passerby, crocheting sweaters and shawls and scrutinizing the western Kansas sky for troubling weather signs. From this perch, she could also monitor my shenanigans, for each day seemed to bring a new melodrama for two ornery twins—Bobby and Gary Morris—and me, especially as we continued our cliffhanger matinees with Mrs. Dessie Batchman.

Mrs. Batchman lived alone in the house next to Grandma's. The house was set back from the street and hid behind overgrown rose bushes gone wild, creeping up the sides of her cottage. Her basement windows, covered with soot, were the only means we had to peek inside to her life and invent our newest adventure.

Mrs. Batchman, in our imagination, was a tiny hunchback wretch whose wire-rimmed glasses wickedly mesmerized anyone younger than twelve, rendering them helpless, of course, against her depravities. Although we rarely saw her, we knew she lured unsuspecting children into her lair and hung them by their ankles from the preserves shelves in her basement. After all, we hadn't seen the Yardley sisters since our last episode of cowboys and Indians when the Morrises dropped their BB guns and I forgot my Hopa-long Cassidy six-shooters when we fled, shrieking from the Batchman house on Halloween.

We also knew that she buried the bodies in her garden, because the tall plants that towered above the others were red with blood. Only later did I learn that the plants were rhubarb. Mrs. Batchman even tried to get us to participate in her ghastly cover-up by giving my Grandma stalks of the plant to put in pies. For that reason, I did not eat rhubarb until well into my twenties. Better to be safe than cannibalistic.

One of my earliest and strongest recollections with Grandma was sitting in those rocking chairs and talking about Shakespeare, Dickens, or how to take a trick in canasta. She would artfully select the reading—perhaps *A Midsummer Night's Dream* or *Oliver Twist*—whatever she thought would suit my mood or the questions I was peppering her with. And then, we would talk like grown-ups about the stories to the rhythmic creaking of the rockers. The creaking seemed to stimulate the introspective juices and helped me struggle with the meaning of the stories and their relevance at that point in my life, even at a time when most boys my age were playing hide-n-seek or drawing rescues on the TV for *Winky Dink*. No answer was ever wrong; just a starting point for deeper Socratic-like inquiry. The fragrance of her lavender sachet mixed warmly with the musty leather volumes, creating the perfect atmosphere for Grandma and grandson.

One spring day, Grandma saw me rocking alone on the porch—pensive, sad. She sat down in the chair next to me and we rocked together for a few minutes, not speaking. Finally, she asked what was wrong.

"I'm worried about growing old," I said.

"Growing old? You're only eight. Why would you worry about growing old?"

"It's not about me. I'm worried about you growing old," I confessed. "I don't want you to grow old."

She hugged me close, then got up and went to her bookcase. She came back with a volume from her Robert Browning collection. She hadn't given me any of his poems to read before, but thought I was ready for one now.

"Read this poem, "Rabbi Ben Ezra," and then come back later this morning and we'll talk."

I remember not understanding most of it, but the first verse was idyllic:

> *Grow old along with me!*
> *The best is yet to be,*

The last of life, for which the first was made:
Our times are in His hand
Who saith "A whole I planned,
Youth shows but half; trust God: see all, nor be afraid!"

We reasoned together later that morning about the beauty of growing old, of its gracefulness and sagacity. She let me discover the wonder of aging—the opportunity for wise counsel to children, the advantages of reflection for the benefit of others, its obligation to pass empathy to the next generation.

"Youth see no further than the end of their noses," she would say, "but grandparents, especially grandmas, see the future."

December 1954

Grandma Younkin's house sat on the busy corner of Lakin and Morton. The white-shingled house was a shotgun affair that stacked living room, dining room, kitchen, and out-quarters in descending order from east to west. The lavishly-carved brass mechanical doorbell had French flowers and scrollwork and made an obnoxious grating sound when the lever was turned clockwise. It was centered in the ornately carved wooden door, and, ironically, would be the one keepsake every grandchild wanted when Grandma sold her house years later.

The living room functioned as the central hub of family activity. A rugged olive chenille couch was tucked neatly under the east picture window with the matching love seat, ottoman, and rocking chair angled around a tear-drop Tiffany floor lamp on the south wall. Queen Anne floral matching chairs sat on either side of the two glass-covered bookshelves that housed the sacred leather volumes of Dickens, Tennyson, Browning, and Shakespeare. The sight-line of all the furniture pointed to the room's focal point—the RCA Victrola floor radio console. Most evenings, the family would gather round the Victrola after dinner to listen to the Elmer Davis newscast, the hilarity of Jack Benny, the spookiness of *The Shadow*, or the inanity of *Fibber McGee and Molly*. That the imagination required of radio listening stimulated more creativity than television viewing (hence, "boob-tube") would not become obvious to any of us until years later.

The dining room was off-limits to anyone under the age of sixteen, and even then could only be used by Grandma's permission. In it were the Kellogg upright piano, the formal walnut dining table, chairs and hutch, and the walnut desk and chair. On the desk, arranged in no particular order, was the black Southwestern Bell telephone, the family bills tray, my bronze baby shoes with the Parker Zephyr fountain pen, and a Webster's Dictionary. The room was kept lightless except for piano lessons, phone calls, and significant family gatherings like birthdays and holiday dinners, which were always presided over by Grandma.

Separating these two rooms, and in the pathway so that it could not be averted, was a large cast iron floor grate housing the gas-fired furnace, menacing for its roiling heat and murmurous groan. When working in winter to heat the entire house, the hot cast iron could melt the soles of Keds in sixty seconds. It was an object to bless and sometimes to curse.

My brother, Charlie, was a pest. Four years younger than me, he wasn't allowed out of the house alone without "someone's" supervision—by default, mine. Looking back on this event, I can state in my defense that seven-year-old boys do not possess the patience to supervise toddlers.

One January day, four inches of fresh-fallen snow beckoned the Morrises and me to build an igloo in their backyard. Dad was at work, Mom was at bridge club, and Grandma was baking. So, Charlie was my annoying responsibility—again.

He brought me his green snow suit, rubber boots, and mittens with the string that connected glove-to-glove. I threaded the mittens through the arms of the coat, snapped the boots tight, secured the correct fingers into the mittens, and started to leave. He cried. I hadn't buckled the coat. I buckled. He cried again because his stocking cap covered his eyes. I uncovered. He cried yet again, grabbing my arm, and I shoved him. He screamed. And I turned to see him lying belly-down on the cast iron grate, wallowing helplessly like an upside-down turtle.

After what seemed like an eternity, Grandma and I lifted him off the grate. The checkered imprint of the grate burned through the coat, through his sweater and undershirt, and into his stomach. His piercing screams echoed in my ears.

Grandma called for an ambulance, which soon whisked Charlie and her to the hospital where they met Dad and Mom. I was left at home alone. What would Dad do to punish me for my transgression? Would Mom trust me again with anything? Would I be allowed to play with Charlie? Would Grandma still love me?

Charlie, my parents, and Grandma came home later that day. Fortunately, the coat and sweater had diminished the searing effect of the furnace from severer injury. But, he was now branded on the tummy with a tic-tac-toe board—something he was peculiarly proud of.

I deserved punishment. My insensitivity and selfishness caused Charlie's injury. Justice demanded it. Dad, however, gently scolded me, wanting me to understand my importance as a big brother. Mom held Charlie and me together, Charlie weeping and blubbering that he was sorry. He was sorry? Grandma held my hand, knowing how ashamed I was.

Forgiveness. Mercy. Not punishment?

I didn't understand.

November 1998

The tall grass in the backyard left tracks of critters trailing under the small wooden bridge. The ornery raccoon perched nervously on the wood railing, seeming to orchestrate an odd parade of squirrels and chipmunks away from Mel's Abyssinian cat, Brutus. Brutus was lurking somewhere nearby. I monitored this scene from the large picture window in Mel's office each week, and found the give-and-take of predator versus prey intriguing. I rooted for the raccoon to lead the other animals to safety.

Soon, Mel entered.

"What have we learned since our last meeting?"

I always wondered whether he intentionally invited me into his office five minutes before he entered so that I might learn some lesson from the backyard scene, a kind of psychiatric Aesop tutorial.

I'd cried often the week before, curled up in the fetal position on the basement couch covered in blankets, sweating profusely. Damien's insidious voice shamed me as I sat like a frightened child in a solitary oak chair in a windowless basement room of an abandoned farmhouse. A bald lamp shined above me, creating a halo of light and shadow that made it difficult to see him as he asked his wearisome questions: "Why did you forget…why did you fail…who do you think you are…how could you?" I had no answer, the questions endless, addled, and lurid.

Mel wondered whether Damien could be my father.

"No."

"Well, could he be like your father?"

"No. My Dad's nothing like Damien," I snapped.

"Well, why do you think Damien's voice triggers your worst episodes?

Over the next forty-five minutes, Mel and I talked about my father, his love of Tommy Dorsey, Duke Ellington, Stan Kenton, Frank Sinatra, and all things big band and jazz. But, most of all, we talked about Glen Miller. I was raised as much by stories told by woodwinds, brass, and percussion as by adults—"In the Mood," "Hear Comes that Rainy Day," "American Patrol," "Pennsylvania 6-5-0-0-0," "I'll Never Smile Again," and on and on.

"Pennsylvania 6-5-0-0-0," I told Mel. "I broke that record when I was playing with Dad's *Best of Glen Miller* record album. Boy, did he get mad. Never seen him that upset with me"

Why that record? He had hundreds.

July 1956: Purloined Air Caps

Over the next three months, Mel focused our sessions on the childhood events rotating through my memory. The reflections recalibrated my identity to the safe harbor of Grandma and my Dad, restored my self-esteem, and strengthened my confidence that I mattered. That we could laugh at some of those recollections and wince at others taught me a lot.

One such memory was Bobby Robertson and me, both age eight, deciding that we needed air caps on our Schwinn bikes' tires. Where did you go to get those? Sears? Woolworth's *Five and Dime*? Reynold's Hardware Store?

Nope.

Bobby and I were walking our bikes south on Main Street towards Duckwall's and noticed the large variety of air caps on cars parked diagonally: crowns, squares, balls, red, white, black, blue—a plethora of air caps of every shape, texture, color, and size. Over the next hour, our penchant for air caps magically exploded into a grocery bag of several hundred. Finding new kinds of these things was addictive.

Triumphantly carrying the bag back to my house like Indiana Jones with a trove of Incan treasures, Bobby and I presented our hoard to my Dad, who asked the obvious question—the one we hadn't anticipated: "Where did you get those?"

We stuttered, glanced at each other, grinned sheepishly and said, "We found them in the alley."

"No, you didn't. Put them back."

"Put them back?"

"Yes. Now."

Dad had the ability to admonish calmly and quietly in a manner that conveyed urgency. So, Bobby and I trudged back to Main Street to begin the arduous task of replacing over two hundred caps on capless cars. Many cars had left their spaces, others had recently arrived, and many were fully capped. We decided early on not to worry about matching the caps correctly and to just put an air cap on each capless tire.

We'd completed a two-block stretch on the east side of Main Street and were starting south on the west side when we noticed a white car parked horizontally behind the cherry-colored Edsel we were presently capping. The car door opened and shut, and the hard sound of heavy footsteps neared. We looked up from our hasty screwing to see the imposing image of a large Great Bend police officer.

"What are you boys doing?" he inquired.

"Putting air caps back on tires," I meekly replied.

"Putting back?"

"Yes, sir."

"Really. Come with me."

Officer Krupke ushered the two of us into the back door of his patrol car.

"What are your names?"

We responded.

"Where do you live?"

We responded fearfully, now knowing we were doomed.

Bobby was taken to his house first. The large officer led the tiny Bobby by the hand to his front door. Bobby disappeared.

Minutes later, the officer escorted me to the front door of 1301 Morton. He turned the raspy door bell. My Dad opened the door and recoiled slightly to the image of his eight-year old son cowering pitifully next to the large officer.

"Your son was stealing air caps from cars on Main Street. A small theft, but theft nevertheless."

Dad didn't give the officer any context regarding his knowledge about my activity. Putting back apparently looked a lot like taking off. And now, nabbed and arrested, a criminal record at eight. I began to cry as Dad took my hand and closed the door.

The next day, Dad took me to the courthouse where we walked hand-in-hand to the cavernous oak-walled courtroom to appear in front of a black-robed, gray-haired judge. He firmly counseled me to follow the law, obey my father, and stay out of trouble.

"Do you have anything to say for yourself?"

"I'm sorry. Won't happen ever again. I promise."

My own version of *Scared Straight*.

Years later, I learned that the judge was a friend of my Dad and that the two of them arranged the appearance at the courthouse to make a dramatic impression on me about "responsibility and citizenship." It was a teachable moment my Dad could not pass up.

"Your father deeply cared about your character, didn't he?" Mel offered.

"Yes. Character, honor, and humility were very important to him."

"You're right. Damien is nothing like your father. You see that, don't you?"

I nodded.

And then he added, "Don't listen to Damien's voice."

May 8, 2011: Dad's Honor

My Dad passed away on May 8, 2011. I think of him often—a man who served his country proudly as a Marine medic in World War II , despite having an exemption from the service for farming; who gave up architectural schooling because he believed he should pay the bills for his wife's hospitalization for tuberculosis and the birth of his first child, me, rather than simply (like much of twenty-first century America) not pay the bills; whose sense of honor was such that he gave up smoking in order to pay for his five-year old daughter's piano lessons long before smoking was known to be bad and long before he knew that the five-year old daughter would earn a master's degree in piano performance.

A man who carried a small gold basketball on his keychain until the day he died.

My Dad played basketball for the Sublette High School Larks in 1941. That Sublette basketball team won the Class B state championship by defeating Oliver 46–23. Led by the legendary Otto Schnellbacher, Sublette won their state tournament games by an average of 18 points. Schnellbacher averaged 28 points per game on the way to being named the tournament's most valuable player. He went on to be a two-sport star at the University of Kansas; an All-American football player who later played for the New York Giants; captain of a basketball team coached by Phog Allen. He was widely known as the "double threat from Sublette."

Wyandotte High School won the AA state championship by defeating Salina 36–31. Most newspapers believed that Sublette could have beaten that Wyandotte team– Kansas' own version of David and Goliath, as chronicled in the movie *Hoosiers*. It was rumored that the *Hutchinson News* even tried to stage the game. Legend tells us strange things.

Schnellbacher always deflected the personal glory in favor of his team-mates: Harold Shaver, Vernon Rutledge, Ethan Winters, Roy Leathers, and Hi Baxter—my Dad. Such was his honor, and theirs.

These young men knew the value of hard work, having grown up in the Dust Bowl of southwestern Kansas when mothers covered their children's faces with wet cloths so that they could breathe. They would work the farm throughout the year and practice basketball after school, all the while maintaining their grades. When my brother and I played basketball at Great Bend High School, my Dad demanded that we maintain our grades, or we wouldn't play. A season of tough practices was never an excuse for faltering in our main purpose of going to school—to obtain an education. Playing selfishly or taunting the other team was not tolerated by the coach and was forbidden by Dad as demonstrating a lack of character and displaying poor upbringing.

Like Schnellbacher, the other members of that team forsook two years of their lives to enlist in the military to serve their country during World War II. Although exemptions could have been readily had, they were not chosen. Such were the reasons Tom Brokaw called this "the greatest generation."

My brother, Charlie, and I longed to play in a state basketball tournament just like our father. My teams never made it there, but Charlie's team did once, losing in the first round. The Leavenworth Lady Pioneer basketball teams that I coached made it to the state tournament seven times, taking third in my last year of coaching. My brother and I never won a small gold basketball.

Sometime before Dad passed away, I asked him what was so special about that gold basketball that he would keep it on his key chain for seventy years. Rubbing the small ball with his gnarly, worn fingers, he said it reminded him of the value of hard work and the importance of honor—"excellence with honor," he called it. A constant reminder—for seventy years.

I think of my Dad during this season of polarizing national politics because I don't believe today's youth or middle-aged, for that matter, are built with such honorable stuff. Rather than expose his family budget to strain, he mowed with the same push mower years after our last neighbor had a powered Lawnboy; he made his children think cooking hot dogs on the grill in the backyard was a bigger treat than filet mignon, and that singing songs together after dinner while the four of us washed the dishes was as good as family life got—long before it was done by the Waltons on TV.

Dad fostered his children's dreams by showing in small ways what they could be: by taking his eight-year old son out to the airport to watch planes land because he heard his son, Charlie, once wistfully offer how neat it would be to fly. "Keep the nose up," Dad would say to the pilot, and he and Charlie would wave as the plane took off. Today, Charlie is a Delta pilot, and my Dad's last word to him before he died was, "Keep your nose up."

He modeled for each of his five children how marriages should work by loving and respecting his wife of sixty-four years as much his last day on earth as the first day he saw her on Grandma's porch after World War II listening to Glen Miller's "Pennsylvania 6-5-0-0-0." He never embarrassed her, never spoke ill of her, never treated her with less than respect, and showed his love in small ways every day of their life together.

In my sixty-nine years I cannot recall anyone to have ought against him, never knew anyone that he was beholden to, and never saw him hesitate to help someone in need, whether young or old, rich or poor, black or white, family or not.

My Dad pursued his work as a postman with missionary zeal. This civil service job was, for him, to be performed with the same commitment, attention to detail, and *esprit de corps* as, well, a Marine medic in time of war, and he treated it with as much pride. More than depositing letters in a metal mailbox, he delivered a smile and a kind word at no extra cost, and dozens of residents reported to me that my Dad made their day with such simple gestures. I can recall with amazement that he knew the name and address by memory of every citizen and business in Great Bend, a town of nearly 20,000. Most of us do well to remember the address of our work or our parents.

Damien was not like my Dad.

Halloween 1958

Although Grandma kept telling us to leave Mrs. Batchman alone, the Morrises and I continued the pestering and peeking. During the fall of 1958, it got worse as we enlisted a mob of knee-biting neighborhood kids to join us in our relentless teasing, not knowing that our imaginative horse play was deeply grieving a kindly lady. But Grandma knew, especially as the mob got bigger and louder and ornerier.

One day when we were rocking in Grandma's chairs, Grandma asked me to read a Robert Frost poem, "Choose Something Like a Star." The poem concludes,

> *And steadfast as Keats' Eremite*
> *Not even stooping from its sphere.*
> *It asks a little of us here.*
> *It asks of us a certain height,*
> *So when at times the mob is swayed*
> *To carry praise or blame too far,*
> *We may choose something like a star*
> *To stay our minds on and be staid.*

I asked her why she had given me a poem about a big star and what it had to do with me, anyway. And, "What the heck is an eremite?" Later that day, in Grandma's way of teaching me, we talked about the star's dependability—its unchanging character amid the commotion in the heavens—and how we should be like that star—constant, kind, and honorable, even in the face of a gang's unkindness or a crowd's rowdiness, or the neighborhood's relentless pestering of one person. I needed to be steadfast of character and realize that making fun could be causing profound pain. I needed to have my mind "staid" and do the right thing, even if I was the only one. Grandma urged me to "Choose Something Like a Star."

And when I stopped, so did everyone else. And Mrs. Batchman came back out and we discovered her delightful laughter and her penchant to make sugar cookies for all of us.

A few years later, when I was twelve or thirteen, Grandma and I revisited that poem, and I asked her once again, "What in the heck is an eremite?" This time she gave me Keats' poem "Bright Star," and I discovered that an eremite is a solitary star, shining brightest in the heavens, that calls us to be our better selves, calls us to look up to the beauty of that highest spot where the sky nuzzles against the face of God, and reminds us about the problems with mobs, bullies, fear mongers, and bigots—and calls us to be our better selves.

> So when at times the mob is swayed
> To carry praise or blame too far,
> We may choose something like a star
> To stay our minds on and be staid.

Grandma's lessons involved meaningful conversations, with each of my answers followed by straightforward questions that encouraged me to discover elusive truths. To think. She was, after all, a teacher teaching me to listen to my better self.

August 1959: Leaving a Safe Harbor

I was happy living with Grandma, playing in her neighborhood, and going to Washington Grade School just three blocks from our house. This was home. Billy Franklin, Bobby and Gary Morris, and Nancy Miller—kick-the-can buddies, cowboys and Indians junkies, best friends. Alice Brown, Tim McGee, Bobby Robertson—classmates and pranksters for nine years. A block away was my other Grandma, Mae Higgins. Grandma Higgins and I would watch *Lawrence Welk*, *Paladin*, and *Gunsmoke* every Saturday night. Did life get any better than that?

And then our family moved from Grandma's house to 2305 Franklin, four miles away, where I had to go to Park Elementary School. My friends were still at Washington School, and I was the new kid at Park. I was lonely, afraid, and scared to make new friends, to try out for Park's football team, to join the neighborhood Cub Scouts. Most importantly, Grandma wasn't there. Who would answer my questions? Who would help me make sense of things?

One day I rode my bike all the way over to Grandma's to have a talk about not living with her anymore. Why couldn't we keep living with her? Why did we need to live so far away? Why did I have to make new friends?

Grandma still wouldn't just give me answers. But she did give me another poem to read— "George Gray" by Edgar Lee Masters. She told me to read it and then call her on the phone later to talk about it. She even told me to tell Mom that she would reimburse them for the phone call. Why couldn't she just tell me what to do? Or take me back?

I read the poem through two or three times, and had an idea of what it was about. The narrator was dead, and seemed to be looking at a granite gravestone with his name and birth and death dates etched on it. He was thinking back about his life: the "love [that was] offered him that he shrank from its disillusionment"…"Sorrow knocked at [his] door, but [he] was afraid"…"Ambition called to [him], but [he] dreaded the chances"—all of the missed chances in his life, now gone.

> And then the narrator observes:
> *And now I know we must lift the sail*
> *And catch the winds of destiny*
> *Wherever they drive the boat.*
> *To put meaning in one's life may end in madness,*
> *But life without meaning is the torture*
> *Of restlessness and vague desire—*
> *It is a boat longing for the sea and yet afraid.*

And, as Grandma and I discussed the poem, I began to understand. Finally, Grandma asked me about that "boat longing for the sea." What did I think about the boat floating in the harbor?

And I said, "At least the boat is safe."

And Grandma paused, looked at me softly, and said, "But that's not what boats are built for, is it?"

I had no answer for that one.

Maybe I could try to make new friends. I could also try out for the Park Pirates football team. And I could be the cool new kid at school. That's always fun to be.

How'd Grandma know so much about boats?

December 1960: The Mother Enigma

She sat introspectively in the third row of pews on Christmas Eve at the First Methodist Church's Christmas Vespers, head down with her hands in her lap like she'd just endured the turgidity of a torrential storm and was thanking the Lord for her survival. The sag in her shoulders pronounced exhaustion. And, of course, it should.

Just that afternoon, she'd finished making rag dolls for Nancy and Lori, hemmed pajamas for Charlie and me, decorated the tree with bobbles, balls, and candles that had been in the Younkin family for generations, and baked rhubarb and apple pies for Christmas Day. She made the extra apple pie because I still refused to eat rhubarb. The green and red bubble lights still worked to the astonishment of everyone—lights that her father, Charles Younkin, had purchased at Duckwall's in 1941. Without them, Christmas wouldn't have looked proper in the Baxter home. And now, Lori, Nancy, Charlie, Dad, and I sat left to right next to each other in the third row of pews waiting for Dr. Franklin Edwards' invocation.

My parents called me Lynn, my middle name. I always wondered why. Could I not handle two syllables—Jef-frey? Did they know someone with that name they didn't like? Maybe Mom chose to call me Lynn. I didn't like it. A lot of girls seemed to be named Lynn; I knew two. Maybe Mom wanted a girl instead of me. I never seemed to measure up to my Mom's expectations as her firstborn. Perhaps it was a problem with being the first, or that I bonded with Grandma Younkin so immediately and intimately, or that her anticipations were too extraordinary. I know I was loved, but it was from a distance—

thoughtfully, stoically, and tepid. I was directly linked with her nightmarish tuberculosis ailment that nearly killed her and which ended my Dad's dream of being an architect. I was a symbol of a young couple's lost aspirations.

I never remember sitting on her lap or being held by her. The sepia-toned photos, faded by the years, show Dad holding me, and Grandma, too. But not my mother. I was in family photos, but not with her alone. The one time I re-member her hugging me was when I bought the wood-colored cardboard na-tivity scene at Woolworth's and gave it to Dad and her for my sixth Christmas. It had taken me nine weeks of doing chores for Grandma Higgins and Grandma Younkin to earn the $5.95 to buy it. Even then, I was five cents short, and the store clerk chipped in the nickel because she'd seen me making weekly payments since Halloween. That nativity set that included Joseph, Mary, baby Jesus in a manger, a donkey, and two of the three kings remained in our family long after I graduated from college.

Mom did all the room-mother things for me throughout elementary school, bringing sugar cookies to my class one Friday afternoon each month, helping with the school fair every September, and serving her obligatory year as Den Mother of my Cub Scout troop. I thrilled to see her come into my classroom and beamed at how pretty she was, dressed like she was ready to work at the American State Bank. She would often leave, though, without a hug or kiss on the cheek.

Not until my eighteenth birthday did I truly realize how much she loved and cared for me. That morning I woke up to discover an envelope tucked carefully under my pillow far enough to be secure, but apparent enough to be seen. In it was a poem my mother had written about a quiet young man who strives for excellence in everything, often fails, but never gives up. She titled the poem "Hidalgo" for a young Spanish nobleman who, through determina-tion, triumphs over obstacles and disappointments. *Hidalgo*, it turns out, is me.

April 20, 1999

Rain drizzled constantly under the dank, dark skies of morning, looking more like nightfall than 11:00 A.M., perfectly underscoring, however, my mood and the previous day's headline. Two teenage boys had stalked through Columbine High School in Colorado, murdering thirteen students and staff and wounding twenty others. I hadn't slept the night before, curling into the fetal position and replaying the scenes of the massacre from endless television footage. Although I hadn't heard Damien's voice in months—the trigger that sent me into my most terrifying episodes—last night's fall into the black hole left me sobbing uncontrollably. Mel's backdoor scene provided little calmness. He was alarmed when he saw my ashen face and bruised-looking eyes, clear signs of torment.

Hesitatingly, he asked, "How are you doing today?"

"Not well. I almost didn't come. I knew you'd be disappointed."

"Disappointed? Why?"

"I know what I look like. I knew you'd be disappointed that I went backwards. I knew you'd think it was Damien, and you'd be upset I did something to let him back in. I'm sorry."

"Was it Damien? I thought we took care of him."

"No. It wasn't Damien. It was worse."

"Tell me what you remember."

"When I was watching the TV coverage of the Columbine shootings and all the students who were killed, my wife came into the room and saw tears pouring from my eyes. She turned off the TV, sat down beside me, and showed me the essay about *To Kill a Mockingbird* that Tara got back from Mrs. Parker, and the artwork Olivia did for social studies. She suggested I make a list about the good things going on in my life and compare them to the list of the bad."

"That sounds good. What went wrong?"

I told Mel about not being able to get the tragic deaths out of my mind—the senselessness, the unforgiving nature, and the calculated coldness of two young men. That was the last thing I remembered until I went to sleep and began the mindless fall into the black hole. I couldn't remember much, but what I remembered was Jordan's last wrenching breath at Children's Mercy Hospital and my decision to remove him from the respirator. My decision. I was responsible, and I was wrong.

We spent the next thirty minutes talking about my difficulties with death experiences, my inability to discern "a sage's advice from the ogre's deceit," and began trolling through my best high school memories. These oddly soothed my agitated mind and returned me to thoughtful consideration of where I was and where I wanted to go. Mel would only see me five more times, but this session was a breakthrough for many reasons.

Spring 1965

Great Bend High School sits at the corner of 19th and Morton, occupying a four-square block area on the *Mason-Dixon Line* separating Roosevelt and Harrison Junior High School attendance zones. Somehow, the students of the two junior highs would settle their differences at back-to-school night before their sophomore year and enter the high school together as proud Black Panthers. The blonde brick campus of buildings was constructed in the mid-fifties, and had expanded twice by the time I was a junior in 1964. All this to accommodate the surge of baby-boomers and the addition to the curriculum of the practical arts (*school-speak* for kids who weren't going to college): auto shop, wood shop, home economics, and typing.

Across the street, the city park curled around the Brit Spaugh Zoo, home to a cacophony of monkeys, ducks, alligators, bison, bears, wolves, giraffes, and lions. Spring breezes—what Grandma called "westerlies"—brought the pungent odor of waste from the predators' cages. Mixed with the stench of the feed lot on the edge of town, these smells could be overwhelming if the breeze was right. The hydrangea bushes that lined the perimeter of the high school warded off the stink like an invisible shield.

On this late afternoon in March, my mind was preoccupied with thoughts of Peyton Marlow (not her real name; I didn't want to embarrass her), the teen angel of the junior class. Pert— blonde, teeth like Sandra Dee's. Peyton froze every room she walked into with her uncommon beauty and a whiff of light cologne that trailed her like a royal cape. She sat beside me in chemistry and made it impossible to concentrate on the formulas, experiments, and lectures of Lester Spong. Lester Spong, with the coke-bottle lenses in his wire rim glasses. Lester Spong, with the starched white shirts and endless supply of ugly bow ties. Lester Spong, with that ever present toothless grin that said, "I'm smarter than all of you put together, so don't try anything."

That day, I sat with head on hands training my eyes on Lester Spong's experiment but allowing my mind to race with fantasies of things to do with Peyton Marlow. Suddenly, a *phzzz* broke the bored silence of the lab. Heads dropped from crooked elbows, snapping the room to attention.

"What was that?" Terry Claassen, my lab partner, asked.

"I don't know; maybe it'll happen again," I answered.

Terry had the brains of Einstein and the looks of Opie Taylor. Standing at 6'0" and weighing 135 pounds, he looked like the Geico lizard with the voice of Darth Vader. The juxtaposition hollered for laughter every time he spoke.

Phzzz. It happened again. Lester Spong appeared to drop a tiny piece from a bar of soap into a beaker of water, producing the magical *phzzz.*

"Wow, that's crazy," Terry whispered. "What was that?"

Lester Spong cleared his throat, directing the attention from the magical beaker to his bulbous black, bespeckled pupils. He wanted us perplexed and unsatisfied more than he wanted us curious. But, as the bell rang, Terry and I were being tugged by curiosity.

"What would happen if you dropped a whole brick of that stuff in a tub of water?" Terry wondered.

"Wouldn't you like to find out?" I replied. And the tug of curious sparked the larger consideration of how we could make this happen.

We knew where Lester Spong kept the enchanted soap. We even knew its name—potassium. We knew when Lester Spong wasn't in his lab—fifth period, when he met Aline Schmitt, the typing teacher, for coffee in the teachers' lounge. But we didn't know if the glass cabinet that housed the phzzz-making brick was locked. Our heist would take serious reconnaissance.

The next day during chemistry, Terry bumped Colleen Bryant into the glass cabinet. It was not an aggressive act, just enough to check if the knob of the cabinet's door was secure. It was not locked. Colleen smiled at Terry, not understanding that the bump was merely a ruse and not an invitation to anything more. Opie Taylor was only attracted to girls with freckles.

Later that afternoon, we struck when Lester Spong was chatting with Mrs. Schmitt. I stood guard at the entrance of his lab, pretending to check my Pee-Chee for algebra notes while Terry slipped into Lester's room for an entire brick of the soap-like object.

Mission accomplished.

The end-of-school bell rang and Terry and I rushed out the south doors of the high school toward his house, which adjoined the football practice field—a perfect coexistence of space and time for the final steps of our plot.

We searched his yard for a container big enough to hold a substantial volume of water. The geranium pot, too small. His sister's swimming pool, too large. The empty aquarium, too fragile. The large, forty-gallon trash barrel, just right. Our Goldilocks machinations complete, we lugged the barrel across the street and into the middle of the practice field. We didn't know what to expect when soap brick met water, but we certainly didn't want to gamble on damaging any part of Terry's house. Mrs. Claassen would kill us.

We dragged the water hose across the street to the barrel and commenced to fill it up. Five gallons, ten, twenty, thirty. Why not all the way to forty? The water-filled barrel stood there waiting for our experiment to begin.

Standing near the curb, at least fifty feet away, Terry and I took turns tossing the brick like horseshoes toward the barrel. Missed. We took three steps closer. Missed again. Three more steps. Still missed. The pressure of hitting the target merged with the stress of doing something evil, and it played havoc with our aim. Finally, in frustration, Terry, brick clutched in his thin hand like Julius Erving with a basketball, loped up to the barrel and dunked it forcefully.

KABOOM!

The water gushed like Old Faithful a hundred feet into the air, buckling the trash barrel sides outwardly so that the barrel squished like a flattened soda can. I hit the ground stunned, then looked up and saw Terry weaving drunkenly toward me, sopped from head to toe. Terry staggered across the street, stumbled on the curb, narrowly missed decapitating himself on the clothesline, and retreated into the safety of his house.

I remained on the ground, the sole criminal in the Lester Spong heist. Who knew that the proclivities of potassium were so calamitous?

Seconds later, the practice field filled with students, teachers, administrators, and Lester Spong. I was ushered to the office like Public Enemy No. 1.

"Who helped you do this?" Mr. Halbower, the principal, asked.

I stood mute, refusing to divulge Terry's name. I may have been a bomber, but I was no snitch.

Mr. Halbower stood 6'6" and was a retired Marine with the physical presence of Ares, the Greek god of war. He could turn miscreant students into quivering blubber with a single fixed stare. Mr. Halbower also attended the First Methodist Church with my family, and I knew full well that my parents would know about today's incident before I got home. Own up to it, beg for mercy, allow a scourge of locusts to infest my body with sores. Anything to gain my freedom by May eighth and the junior-senior prom.

Go down, Moses. Let my people go.

I argued that this was the only time I'd appeared in the principal's office for anything unvirtuous during my two and a half years at Great Bend High School. I was unlikely to do anything like this again. Five years of watching *Perry Mason* had given me the tools for cajoling a successful plea agreement from my parents: five weeks of being grounded on weekends, no telephone calling, and a written apology to Lester Spong. That would be the hardest part. I wasn't sorry.

I wondered how I would be received at school.

Before I got to chemistry class the next day, the potassium heist had taken on legendary proportion. Terry pledged allegiance to me for not having ratted him out, fellow juniors urged me to run for senior class president, and Peyton Marlow sent a note that smelled of Estee' Lauder, hoping I would ask her to prom. Who knew that the junior class answer to Brigit Bardot pined for someone like Pretty Boy Floyd?

Terry graduated the next year at the top of the GBHS Class of 1966 and matriculated to Dartmouth College on full scholarship before getting his law degree at Georgetown. We talked from time to time and reminisced at high school reunions—until our thirtieth year. Terry was killed in a plane crash with his son, Ben, in upstate New York when he was returning Ben to college from fall break.

I hadn't thought about the potassium explosion event for many years; in fact, not until the day I heard of Terry's death. And now it seemed like my only memory of Terry from high school. That, and how he signed my Rhorea Yearbook: "Never forget our wonderful friendship."

I would discuss Terry's death with Mel several times over the next few months.

Together, we reckoned that life's trivial moments sometimes bear significance in disproportion to their merit. They remind us that humanity resides in minute details, unique experiences separating each of us from the other by poignant moments locked away in the brain's scrapbook waiting to be recalled at the oddest time. Sometimes our mischievous selves win out over the parental strictures of being a good boy. And that isn't necessarily a bad thing.

KABOOM.

October 1965: Twelve Minutes

The halo of lights enclosed the Great Bend High School football stadium in a haze of frenzied activity. Cheerleaders shimmied in below-the-knee skirts to the throbbing beat of the marching band blasting the school fight song. Forty-three confident black-clad Panther football players jogged onto the field while Hutchinson Salt Hawks, Hays Cadets, and Garden City Buffaloes mugged and trash-talked at the more athletic Panthers running by them to their own sideline. Each of those games ended in resounding losses to the Panthers, ranked number one in Kansas for the first time in school history. Only the Dodge City Red Demons were able to mar an otherwise spectacular 8–1 season.

Great Bend was led by two All-Staters. The defense, anchored by Randy Keller, mauled opposing offenses, holding seven of its nine opponents scoreless. Zero. A single wing offense shattered the West Central Kansas League rushing record with Keller pancaking opposing tackles and linebackers for the swift and agile Black Panther tailback.

I can remember one game when the score was close at the end of the third quarter. Fatigued bodies strained for rejuvenation. Twelve minutes of bone-crunching, bruise-bonking body slams remained. The Black Panther tailback took a direct snap from center. He hurdled a lunging lineman, zigzagged around a linebacker and cornerback, and sprinted untouched for sixty-five yards into the end zone.

After he'd carried the ball more than thirty times.

After having played almost every down on offense and defense.

Against one of the best defensive teams in the state.

It was the most breathtaking display of power and speed I've ever seen. Ever. Randy Yowell, Great Bend High School Black Panther. All-state running back. Ornery prankster. Fellow Beatles junkie. Dear friend.

This was my first recollection of Randy after Sharen, our senior class secretary, told me that Randy died two days before of a massive heart attack. He'd become a shell of the friend I'd known—broken, bloated, and besieged by demons of his own making.

Randy and I were born on the same day (January 21) in the same year (1948), but in different hospitals. We came to believe we were fated to be a dynamic duo. Randy was a carbonized willow-wisp of a human being, coiled so tightly that he exploded from point A to point B on command, powerfully and gracefully. Blue eyes, sandy red hair, and v-shaped face, he always had the look of satisfied expectation. Randy was, and is, the best pure athlete I've ever seen. What happened on his journey from that football game to the day he died? Did anyone know about his struggles? Did anyone help him? Where was I?

Jon Briel, Terry Mohr, Randy, and I were a sight to behold in 1965. The Beatles had recently come to America, and "Can't Buy Me Love" and "I Wanna Hold Your Hand" were either playing on our transistor radios or being mimicked by us in our best falsettos. We dressed in pointy Robin Hood-type shoes, tight sharkskin pants, and paisley shirts in homage to these British invaders. When that wardrobe ran out, we wore Levis, t-shirts, and canvas Converse Chuck Taylors. We were nothing if not fashionable. But Randy always looked the best, in a James Dean cool kind of way.

One of our favorite pastimes was sneaking into the St. Rose Catholic Church gym to play basketball, especially in the icy chill of winter. We'd gather outside the large windows of the basement gym, raise the unlocked window carefully, and then sidle down the heating vent that ran from ceiling to the floor in the northwest corner of the gym. The Jesuit nuns were busy preparing meals or ministering to parishioners or needling rosaries—occupied with obligations that kept them from the echoing chambers of the basketball court. We never dribbled the ball (just passed it crisply), never shot the ball off the backboard (that received deductions in points), and never cried out in delight or grief about any play. The games were played exuberantly but silently for fear of being evicted. Only years later did we learn that Sister Mary Barbara left that particular window open throughout the winter to give us a safe place to play.

Randy's passing was shocking—one of those life events you can't escape and yet don't want to forget. He'd developed liver and heart problems from years of heavy smoking and drinking, had ballooned to nearly 300 pounds, and suffered from diabetes. He talked often to his brother, Skip, about poor decisions made, opportunities missed, and the inability to pick up the pieces and put them back together again.

In his last call to Sharen, he told her about the stuff the four of us got away with—our adventures and misadventures, our triumphs and disasters, and the bonds of friendship that had grown faint with the passing years. He wished we could reconnect; he longed to let us know how splendid those times were for him, the orneriest prankster in the bunch. Two weeks later, he was gone. I wish I had been there for him.

For now, I'll remember Randy and the way he was in that football game— slashing, dashing, glorious; when his will and his wile could be summoned effortlessly, when his best self was shared by us all, and when opportunity was always just a breath away.

September 1966: Finding Connie

She was out of my league. We met the fall semester of our freshman year at the University of Kansas. I was a mediocre basketball player, but with the best seat in Allen Fieldhouse to watch the legendary Jo Jo White turn explosive basketball skills into ballet. She was the runner-up to Miss Kansas the year Miss Kansas became Miss America. I was awed—the most beautiful and composed woman I'd ever seen.

Blonde, blue-eyed, petite, with a graceful walk and gracious smile, she took my breath away with "hello" at the Alpha Kappa Lambda–Delta Gamma luncheon. I have no remembrance of our conversation, although I'm sure I babbled a lot. Two weeks later, I finally worked up the nerve to call her. She came to the phone, said "hello," and I—I hung up. Two weeks later, I worked up the courage to call her again. She came to the phone, said "hello," and I—I hung up again.

This dance continued for three years.

Frankie Valli and the Four Seasons sang a song that could have been my anthem for this young woman—

My eyes adored you, though I never laid a hand on you, my eyes adored you—so close and yet so far away.

We met again at a fraternity/sorority function our junior year. I was nervous that she might recognize my voice and discover that I was the one phone-stalking her, but then remembered that as soon as she said "hello," I hung up.

We talked pleasantly about her starring roles in KU musicals, the KU Orange Bowl football team, KU basketball, and campus life in general. I was still dazed by her, but apparently not the freshman dweeb I'd been. I came out of this meeting with a date—our first. She asked me to the Delta Gamma Pinafore Party.

We dated for several months. Movie dates, occasional lunches or dinners, a concert or two. Nothing serious. Would it ever be?

Finally, one summer morning I walked across campus to see her at the DG house. We hadn't seen each other for several days, and I wanted to talk with her about our relationship and whether it was going anywhere. Just to be sure I said the right things, acted non-dweebily, and garnered the Good Lord's backing; I stopped to pray at Danforth Chapel, a cozy, ancient limestone sanctuary on the edge of the KU campus.

And, as I walked in the back door, Connie walked in the front. Epiphany. Today I picture angels singing the "Hallelujah Chorus" from the church rafters—a kind of heavenly blessing.

Her parents, especially her step-father, didn't believe I was worthy of her. To be honest, I wasn't sure either. But we grew closer; her strengths supported my weaknesses, my strengths supported her weaknesses, and together we were better human beings than we were separately. Eighteen months later, I proposed. It was the most heart-rending, stressful thing I've ever done. I feared what her answer would be.

Forty-six years later, my eyes still adore her. From the death of our first child, Jordan, to the birth of our first granddaughter, Avery, I've seen Connie's beauty take on deeper significance. She's blessed our three children with attention to detail, determined accountability, and compassionate character that has indelibly marked each of them. Although their livelihoods are different—audio engineer and autistic counselor, Black Hawk helicopter pilot and mother, human resources manager and favorite aunt—they are uniquely and ubiquitously marked by their mother.

With all of my foibles and flaws, she has encouraged, needled, praised, scolded, and blessed me into the person I am today. Several years ago, when I was unable to walk the quarter mile to the swimming pool with our grandson, Hunter, because of the pain in my knees from weighing four hundred and sixty pounds, Connie sensed my shame. She began researching the ways I should consider getting my health back and rediscover the true me beneath the obesity. She found the YouTube videos, made appointments with experts, and helped me find a way. When we were going to be late for a seminar with a prospective surgeon, it was Connie who insisted on continuing. This surgeon turned out to be the one we trusted, and the one who did the surgery.

She is still out of my league.

1971: First Year of Teaching

I did my student teaching at West Junior High in Leavenworth. After eight weeks of working with ninth graders under the watchful tutelage of the ancient Mrs. Weaver, I believed I was ready to teach anyone anything. Since I'd finish student teaching in mid-October, I planned to substitute until I got a full-time job the next year. So I thought. On that third Friday in October 1971, Mrs. Weaver announced:

"An English teacher at Immaculata High School is going to Korea with her husband. How would you like to start teaching Monday?"

Hmm. Finish student-teaching on Friday, teach real students on Monday. I could do this.

On Monday, I showed up at Immaculata High School ready to teach. I assigned Nathaniel Hawthorne's "Young Goodman Brown." It was in the junior textbook, these were juniors, I loved Hawthorne, and I expected them to read and understand the story—just like the students in *Room 222*. I was shocked the next day when the class sat mute in response to my question, "What did you think about Hawthorne's story?"

Silence.

"Anyone?"

More silence. "Really?"

This same scenario continued for two weeks. I was doing class like Professor Haugh taught me at KU and like Mrs. Weaver modeled when I student taught. Why wasn't this working? My stomach churned, my palms sweat, my heart raced, and panic attacks began.

I called my Grandmother, a retired English teacher. Her advice was simple. She took me back to the times we would discuss literature in her rocking chairs on the front porch, when I'd pose questions and she'd suggest answers that could be found in great literature. Calling my attention to *Hamlet*, she counseled, "Remember who you are."

I needed to be me—not Professor Haugh or Mrs. Weaver. Me. My love of literature did not carry over to students by osmosis. I needed to help them discover the issues and themes that would make their reading—well, meaningful. I promised those students, as I have every other class since then, that if I couldn't justify an assignment, we wouldn't do it.

Remember who you are; but there were more lessons to learn.

Immaculata High School sat catty-corner from the Davis Funeral Chapel. One warm November morning, I was doing a writing activity with my juniors and working one-on-one as much as I could. I'd opened the windows, and you could feel the gentle breeze. It was a marvelous moment.

Suddenly, I heard Tony screaming something inaudible. As I turned, I could see Tony hanging halfway out the window, balanced like a fulcrum, yelling toward the funeral home, "Hey, bud, who you buryin' today?"

I was petrified. I raced to grab him by the belt and pull him back into the classroom. Just then, Sister Mary Jo (the principal, and a nun who closely resembled a pit bull) scurried into the room, eyes blazing, complexion flushed red, spewing smoke through her nose. I knew I was in trouble. "I'll see you later," she whispered to me as she passed by, holding Tony by the ear.

As it turns out, teachers really do need eyes in the back of their heads, but apparently those aren't issued until the teacher is tenured. I replayed that morning again and again, trying to figure out what I could have done. She's going to suspend me or fire me—or yell at me. And as I thought about the scene, I began to chuckle—the whole thing made me chuckle until I laughed out loud. And then I knew what I needed to do.

I got Tony after school and took him with me to the funeral home where we apologized. The funeral home owner was polite and so impressed with how Tony and I handled our apology that he called Sister Mary Jo to brag about her wonderful students and teachers.

In *Inherit the Wind*, Henry Drummond, a lawyer, observes, "When you lose your power to laugh, you lose the power to think straight." My laughter helped me to think straight and resolve a bad situation.

Remember who you are and trust your sense of humor. What else did I need to know?

One particular student, David weighed heavily on my mind the whole year. At 6'5" and 150 lbs., he looked like Ichabod Crane and dressed like a hippie. David would not do assignments, would not discuss the reading, would not work with others. Nothing.

I was in my room grading papers one April day after school and listening to James Taylor sing "Fire and Rain." David peaked in the door and asked what I was doing. It was the first time I'd heard his voice.

Did I like James Taylor?

"Yeah, James Taylor got me through college."

"How about Jack Johnson?"

And we began a long talk about guitars and thoughtful lyrics. And, with that, I began to find ways to make the poetry and stories I assigned to my students more relevant. David began to participate. He even shared some of his own poetry. I showed him how his poetry reminded me of Emily Dickinson and Langston Hughes. He smiled.

Several weeks later, David shared a poem about his senior class. He wondered if he could share it with some of his classmates. We did, and his poem was so well-liked that they wanted him to read it at graduation. David practiced and polished and memorized it.

Two days before graduation, David drowned in the Missouri River. The seniors dedicated graduation to him, and the class president read his poem.

Every time now that I have a student who doesn't participate, who disrupts the class, who fails to turn in assignments, I think of David. David taught me that every student is capable of great things. Every one of them. I might not see the light go on like I did with David, but I'm persistent and encouraging.

These are the three things I learned in my first year of teaching: you cannot teach like anyone else but you; develop a sense of humor; and build relationships with your students. The three things other teachers learn in their first year might be different. But, whatever you learn, it's part of your journey to becoming a good teacher. I've also learned that the best thing you can do for your students is provide hope. Whether the student is disruptive, arrogant, immature, intelligent, wealthy, or poor, teachers are first and foremost agents of hope.

In *The Shawshank Redemption*, Andy writes Red a thoughtful letter about starting a new life. His letter concludes, "Remember that hope is a good thing, maybe the best of things. And, no good thing ever dies."

1978: Jordan

Jordan Lance Baxter was born the evening of February 22, 1978, in St. John Hospital in Leavenworth—the first grandchild of Hi and Pat Baxter and Donald and Myrna Zenor, and the eleventh great-grandchild of Grandma Younkin. The pressure for Connie and me to have this special child had been building for the seven years of our marriage, and the time had come to satisfy everyone's expectations.

Connie was teaching choral music at West Junior High and I was an English teacher and basketball coach at Leavenworth High School. All signs for a healthy birth were consistently good with each doctor's appointment: weight, heart, activity, ten fingers, ten toes, check, check, check. Due Date: March 5. All systems go.

In the middle of the school day on February 18, Connie's contractions were such that we made a run to the hospital, just to be on the safe side. Braxton-Hicks contractions, the nurses called it. "False labor" is was what the head nurse translated. And the maternity staff seemed to chuckle behind the counter about the naiveté of this young couple.

Mid-day February 22, the contractions began again, this time more strongly. I raced to pick Connie up at West and then rushed to the hospital. Braxton-Hicks again. The doctor met with us to allay our concerns and encourage us about the health of the baby. He then gave Connie a painful pelvic exam and explained our alternatives.

Minutes later, Connie started another series of contractions, stronger and more rapid. For the next four hours, labor pains mounted in intensity and speed. Finally, at 11:33 P.M., after being at St. John Hospital for ten hours, Jordan Lance Baxter was born. At five minutes, his APGAR score was six; at ten minutes it was seven. Jordan Lance was healthy.

We called both sets of parents, who were at once joyful and relieved. They planned to make the trip to welcome this most precious child into the family the next day. Connie and I were both exhausted and knew we needed sleep. The next day would be a well-wishing extravaganza. I went home and collapsed in our bed, giddy with excitement that a son, grandson, and great grandson was added to the family.

Three hours later, the phone rang. I answered, somehow knowing that this was not a call I wanted. The nurse said to get to the hospital quickly, that the baby was struggling. I don't remember how I dressed, don't remember driving to the hospital, and don't remember how I got into the hospital. I only remember a yellow haze clouding my vision, hovering thickly over my thoughts.

I wheeled Connie down to the maternity's emergency room to see Jordan in the incubator. He was wired and tubed so unartfully that it was difficult to see his tiny body. His small chest puffed and unpuffed, puffed and unpuffed, then stuttered and shivered, paused, and then puffed and unpuffed. Hyaline Membrane Syndrome, the nurse called it. I knew the word "hyaline" was the Greek word *hyalos*, meaning crystal. "Crystal membrane" sounded almost like a good thing, but medically described the color of the membrane that was preventing Jordan from breathing normally.

St. John did not have the pediatric experts or the medical equipment to help Jordan. The closest hospital to provide the needed care was Children's Mercy Hospital, thirty-five miles away. Before Jordan could be transported by ambulance, though, he would need to stabilize.

Connie and I sat in her hospital room, barely able to look at each other, unable to carry on a conversation, together but alone in our own sense of failure. How could this be happening in America? Chinese women give birth to healthy children in rice paddies. How could we not do this?

Periodically over the next five hours, the emergency technicians from Children's Mercy would give us a report about Jordan's status and whether we could now make an ambulance run. Finally, at 9:15 A.M. the emergency doctor determined that we must make the run for Jordan to have a chance. I remember driving behind the ambulance and arriving at Children's Mercy, but I have no recollection of anything in between. Thirty minutes later, the doctor came into the waiting room and motioned me into his office.

Jordan was hooked to a respirator, which was keeping his heart beating erratically. He'd suffered tremendous brain damage and organ failure, but the respirator could keep his heart beating indefinitely. The doctor said I must make the decision of what to do.

"Is Jordan in pain?"

"Yes."

"Could he get better?"

"Very doubtful."

"Can I see him?"

"Sure."

And for a few short moments, I stared through thick tears at my son struggling to breathe, puffing and unpuffing, fighting for each breath, unsuccessfully. A precious child straining for each gulp of oxygen, clinging to the prayerful hope of the Baxter family. My breath, just like Jordan's, labored. How could I be expected to make a decision like this? How could joy turn to despair so quickly?

"Mr. Baxter, I need you to make a decision."

I gave the doctor permission to remove the respirator. And then, with three raspy breaths, Jordan silenced.

Later that morning when I got back to St. John Hospital, I sobbed as I told Connie, "Jordan passed away, and I'm—and I'm responsible."

Jordan Lance Baxter was buried in the children's circle at Mount Muncie Cemetery. His funeral was attended by aunts, uncles, parents, grandparents and students from the high school and the junior high. Connie's choir students, led by Bobby Lang, sang a beautiful arrangement of "Amazing Grace."

Nearly forty years later, the memory of Jordan's short life still fills my eyes with a juxtaposition of smiles and tears. Dustin, Tara, and Olivia were all born after him, but all three seem to know Jordan as their older brother. Their lives have been marked by his short life in a special, miraculous way. What would their lives have been like with Jordan as an older brother?

The weight of my decision was crippling.

1979: Dustin

Floppy navy NY Yankees ball cap pulled snuggly over his white-blonde hair, blue eyes fixed fiercely on the target, Dustin Lenn Baxter would launch himself in his toy car down the slalom-like driveway. Twenty-nine, thirty, thirty-one times, and still counting. Like then, what Dustin thrills to passionately, he pursues with full-throttled exuberance.

Born August 21, 1979, Dustin was the boy wonder of our lives. He had no patience with hugging, which tempered the Grandmas' pleasure and left them ill-equipped and starved for holding him on their knees. This grandchild had little time for such annoyances, preferring the outdoors, the inventive games, the worlds to conquer behind each door, each imagined scenario. With particular attention to the best OshKosh fashion, Dustin was the best-dressed of young boys, the ultimate GQ of the single digit set. In kindergarten, he wore a shirt and tie to school each day, emulating Dad, professing seriousness into academia.

Reading, writing, math, soccer, basketball, dodge ball—everything came easily, like he'd intuited the skills and intelligence necessary to achieve them pre-birth. Our hearts broke with each effort, thrilled to see his abilities, his achievements, his records lapsed only by having to come inside for lunch or dinner. Dustin's passions—whether for people or activities or beliefs—seldom take backseat to the mundane necessities of life, like eating and sleeping.

His mother and I have generally allowed our children to discover the sports or activities they wanted to claim as their own, except once for Dustin. His senior year, I encouraged him to practice basketball in the fall and forsake soccer season, the worst and most selfish advice I've given a child of mine, and one that haunts me to this day. Dustin exuded confidence, professed joy, and demonstrated thrill with each move on the soccer field. I will always believe my poor advice about his best athletic endeavor in favor of my chosen sport denied him the opportunity for singular pleasure his senior year. Time may heal all wounds, but forgiveness to fathers drudges doggedly.

Dustin has the intelligence of a NASA scientist, the artfulness of Kandinsky, and the musicianship of Harry Hornsby (inside joke). We love him for his passions, his talents, his integrity. His setbacks will turn into triumphs, his long road to happiness will fill him with the patience and commitment to make a difference; his best part, his best being, is yet to come.

We pray that Dustin know the peace that passes understanding, that he experience the joy of the commonplace, that he be thrilled by things gentle, and that his life's purpose be consistent with being a blessing more than being blessed.

8/2/82: Tara

Tara Elisabeth Baxter—TeeBo to me—was born magically on August 2, 1982, at 8:02 P.M., 8 pounds 2 ounces of vibrating vitality and vim. 8/2/82 at 8:02 at 8 lbs. 2oz.—4 by 8s and 2s. Fortune forewarned by numbers too precise to be coincidental; the God-decreed evidence of a life promised to exceptionality.

Tara seemed to know what she wanted and how to get there within hours of her birth, and only Dustin's theft of her neonatal night cap threatened to alter her mission from God. Like Kunta Kinte, we knew she was God's more than ours, and that we were accountable for her caretaking, temper-mending, and encouragement before she was unleashed on the waiting world, or even a boyfriend.

She credits her attention to detail, her ability to focus on the-thing-at-hand, and her unwavering sense of rightness to monitoring what got Dustin in trouble, and then doing the opposite. She practiced this mantra fastidiously. Tara was always on time, always thorough, always neat, never silly. Whatever she started, she completed; whatever skill she tried, she mastered. Tara was and is scary in her drive to achieve stronger, faster, better.

Tara attacked music the same way; with a vengeance to achieve. The first instrument to receive her wrath was a yellow Fisher-Price tambourine. At the hint of a musical need, Tara would break into a full voice that tethered between shout and on-pitch tremolo, "This is the day that the Lord hath made, let us rejoice and be glad in it," the tambourine banging rhythmically on her left leg. Tara sang with such insistence that her Aunt Nancy once proclaimed that Tara would be smuggling Bibles into Russia before she turned eighteen.

Until she was married, I only remember her crying twice. The first time, understandably, was when she was three and a firecracker exploded in her hand. The second time, ten years later, was in an Olathe gymnastics meet. In her most troubling event, the balance beam, she slipped off twice, leaving no doubt she couldn't win the meet. I hurriedly hobbled down to the wire separating contestants from parents, put my arms around her shoulders, and encouraged her to "Disregard the insignificance of one mistake and focus on the next three events at hand, and I will be prouder of how you continue than if you'd made no mistake in the first place." Tara scored nine on the bars, on the floor, on the vault, and went on that year to be Missouri State Champion.

The lesson learned then would follow her in diving, pole vaulting, academics, and soldiering. She was a Black Hawk helicopter pilot, a captain—company commander—with the 82nd Airborne, America's strategic response team. Stronger, faster, better. Kind of like smuggling Bibles into Russia.

In many ways, Tara is her mother; the best woman I have ever known. Like her mother, Tara is fiercely loyal, protective of her family, and more demanding of herself than of others. She has the unique knack for dispensing advice and discipline with a velvet-covered sledge hammer—the receiver is righteously upbraided, but left with the knowledge that he or she can improve for the better.

She has mellowed with age, balanced by Trent's (her husband) good humor and practical wisdom as well as the responsibilities that go with mothering Hunter Owen Talley—HOT, in more ways than one; Wyatt Lynn, the intrepid ornery one; and Avery Makenzie, our first granddaughter.

Tara illuminates the way for her family, will not suffer fools, and demands excellence in every task, activity, and mission. I pray that her life will be tempered with patience, fostered with joy, and illuminated by the goodness of those who love her and wish her well.

1987: Olivia

I will be damned forever for uttering, in hopeless exasperation, that Olivia could not be potty-trained. But, I should not be surprised that this younger daughter, who wouldn't talk until she was fourteen months old, couldn't pass beginner's swimming lessons—ever—, and wouldn't potty-train on demand, should become the most social of all of our children, would become captain of her high school swim team, and would one day master the art of serving a gourmet meal to hundreds in a model restaurant with the cleanest bathrooms this side of the Mississippi.

Olivia was born on May 9, 1987, to a family of an older brother who one day tricked her into thinking egg dye pellets were sweet tarts with disturbing results, and an older sister who dressed her like she was a real live Barbie doll every day of her childhood. Somehow, Olivia survived and prospered.

Olivia's tender heart was discernible at a young age, her empathetic radar at work endlessly and fortuitously. Her third grade teacher lauded her for the ability to encourage, hug, and sympathize with her less fortunate, troubled classmates. By osmosis, she could (and still can) understand someone's hurt and form the immaculate strategy to lift the heart, to help the misbegotten see the glass as half full.

But this gift can also be a curse when applied to her. Olivia senses someone's enmity against her and roils readily into drama-queen mode. She lacks the facility to counsel herself. Experience and maturity will bring her the patience, insight, forbearance—hurt's answer to selflessness. A small cure for a wondrous gift.

Olivia has often seen herself in her sister's shadow, measured herself against Tara's achievement, and judged herself harshly in the comparison. Olivia will learn that Tara's achievements, although formidable, are not a valid statistical comparison—touchdowns are not compared to home runs. Olivia achieves because of persistence, often in the face of daunting odds; sheer will power meets brick wall.

Olivia's exuberance is infectious, her humor eclectic, her loyalty unmatched. Whether she realizes it or not, she is God's gift to the downtrodden, the hopeless, the unfortunate. That measure was confirmed in the third grade at Muncie School, on the high school swim team she captained, in her ROTC unit, and in her classwork at MU.

Her goodwill is in the faces of her friends, in the eyes of young Costa Rican children, and in the manners of her nephews Hunter and Wyatt when she celebrates movie night with them. Olivia is a prodigious young woman who has made Mom and Dad proud, and her fulfillment awaits only the self-confidence to achieve greatness.

1988: Connie and the Cyclops

He shouted, "Why don't you sit down, fatty?" I couldn't believe my ears. The big white guy in the Carhartt overalls and NASCAR ball cap was calling someone "fatty." Out loud.

"You—I'm talking to you, fatty," and all the eyes at the Cody Park Soccer Field—ten-year-old Eagles, ten-year-old Bombers, moms, dads, little sisters, big brothers, and referees—stopped and stared my way.

He was yelling at me.

All I'd done was shout "foul" when my own ten-year-old son, Dustin, had been tackled from behind, blind-sided. He lay on the ground hurt for what seemed like sixty seconds, unsure of the extent of his injury. And I instinctively shouted, "foul!"

Apparently Mr. Carhartt-NASCAR was related to the Bomber tackler and took aim at me. "FATTY," he shouted again,

The words and stares sunk into my skin like water soaking into a sponge. My heart pulsed awkwardly, betraying my attempt to act collected and cool. I was fat, after all. Four hundred and sixty pounds of fat—enormous size 7X, 64" waist, waddling-duck, obese. His words were like an indictment of my sinfulness and gluttony. The world turned slow-motion yellow.

Play began again and the sound of kicked and tethered balls picked up tempo. Cheers and shouted directions and sudden huzzahs told the story of youth soccer. The stridency of voices blended into an afternoon symphony of children of all ages and adults of both genders. All, save mine. I dare not speak again.

"C'mon, Dustin," I finally murmured. "You can do it," I muttered louder. "Fatty, fatty, you there. I said sit down," he shouted again.

But, I couldn't sit down, knowing that if I did so, I'd struggle to get back up. I looked for a place to retreat where I could watch the game and silently cheer for my son out of the view of Mr. Carhartt.

I looked for Connie, but she was gone. Had I lost her during my search for seclusion? And then I saw the 5'4" blonde in Eagle mom soccer sweatshirt marching purposefully toward the massive Polyphemus-like Mr. Carhartt. Jabbing her index finger repeatedly into his chest, she barked, "Don't you ever yell at my husband again! He's a better father than you will ever be!"

And the same crowd of ten-year old Eagles, ten-year old Bombers, moms, dads, little sisters, big brothers, and referees who had witnessed my embarrassment now stopped and gaped with approving applause at the bully being rebuffed by a petite soccer Mom.

I smiled for the first time in weeks.

October 12, 1999

The squirrels frolicked in Mel's backyard wilderness, much to the chagrin of the raccoon, chipmunks, and Brutus, Mel's Abyssinian cat. Relentlessly, they toyed with the birdhouse Mel put up for the benefit of the cardinals that considered making a nest nearby. I hated those squirrels.

But watching them somersault, stand on their heads, twist and turn using their tails for balance, all the while trying to get the seed from the birdhouse intended for the cardinals, was captivating. What athletes! If I was to pick an animal soccer team, nine of the eleven members would be squirrels. Persistently, they learned by failing—found a better way, probed for a weakness, and, motivated by a single thought, focused on solution. Aesop would be smiling.

Mel entered his office.

"How are we doing today?"

"Good. I think I'd like to talk about teaching again, if you think I'm ready."

Mel knew that I 'd been unwilling to talk about several matters, but also knew that I needed to talk about them. Traumatic events can be buried deep in one's core and layered with years of excuses, justifications, alibis, and mitigations. The trick is to begin to find the wedge to peel those layers, find the synapses that will start to lay new groundwork to avoid the trigger, or, better yet, run over the trigger. Mel and I had made progress, and now I was willing to talk about Jordan.

"My brother, Charlie, told me something the other day that I never knew."

"What's that?"

"He said he admired my strength. When I asked him what made him think I was strong, he said my reaction to Grandma's death—that he never saw me cry any time before, during, or after her funeral."

"How'd you feel about that?"

"He thought he was giving me a compliment. He wasn't."

We spent the next forty minutes talking about Grandma Younkin and her singular effect on my life, and that I hadn't cried for her, hadn't grieved. The child in me longed for succor, pined for the comfortable smell of Grandma's lavender sachet, the sweetness of her appliquéd hankies, and her sensible wisdom. She nurtured me, created me, and fashioned my heart with the delicacy of language. She taught me that "the best was yet to be."

Jordan was gone, too. I didn't understand death—the end of something, of someone I could hear and touch and smell. And I was responsible.

I looked out the window at the raccoon, chipmunks, and Brutus. They huddled together, expecting a flourish of activity. Then, as the squirrels skittered stealthily up the stanchion that held the birdhouse at its peak, I began to weep peacefully for the first time in years.

Grandma's Final Lesson

For months after Jordan's death, I could barely speak to anyone in my family. In spite of the well-wishes, the soothing sorries, and the caresses of the neck, I was speechless. I wanted nothing to do with comfortable remedies. I made a decision that caused my son's death. I didn't deserve kindness or sympathy.

One Sunday morning, I got a call from Grandma wanting to see how I was doing. I hadn't spoken to her for weeks. I knew she must be disappointed.

We talked for a while about nothing in particular, and then she asked me to read a passage from the Old Testament that she'd had me read years ago, one that I'd forgotten. After reading it, she wanted me to call her back later that afternoon so we could discuss it. Once again, I was with her in those faded green rocking chairs on her front porch.

The passage was from the book of Habakkuk—three small chapters stuck in the middle of a series of small books in the Old Testament. It's by a prophet people know almost nothing about— not his hometown, not his occupation, not even his parentage or tribe. Almost the entire book is written in *chiasmus*, something good literature teachers would recognize.

The passage Grandma wanted me to re-read was from the third chapter:

> *Although the fig tree shall not blossom*
> *Neither shall fruit be on the vines*
> *The labor of the olive shall fail*
> *And the fields shall yield no meat*

The flock shall be cut off from the fold
And there will be no herd in the stalls…

Nothing is going right for Habakkuk. The fig tree is no longer blooming, the vineyards are producing no grapes, harvest time has been a failure, the sheep pens are empty, and the cattle stalls are vacant.

That afternoon I called Grandma back and we talked about the passage. Habakkuk's life is in trouble—failure is all around him. Bad news are his headlines.

"And what does he do—what choice does he make?" asked Grandma. "Look at the next word in the passage."

"Yet."

"That means *nevertheless, notwithstanding…*YET, he says."

I will rejoice in the Lord, I will joy in the God of my salvation.

In the middle of trouble, Habakkuk chooses to affirm the positive; to take his stand on joy. Grandma said I must choose joy, not sorrow. That choice must be made every day; it must be my response to trouble of any kind. Such a choice might be a struggle and might seem too hard to make, but it must be made, because trouble will come.

And with Grandma's counsel, I began to talk with Connie again—earnestly, honestly, openly, and about things that mattered. We began to run again, to perform in musical theatre, to celebrate our life together, and to consider having children again.

Grandma Younkin's life was a blessing. I remembered how she helped me save for and buy the nativity set at Woolworth's Dime Store, how I learned that Skeeter Rayburn's cerebral palsy didn't make him any less wondrous of a human being, why she wouldn't let me buy Eisenhower stamps at the post office, and why eating the salt map I made of Alaska in Cub Scouts was not a good way to celebrate Alaska's statehood.

I remembered when I was eight or nine how Grandma would pull up the foot stool next to the kitchen counter and coach me to crank flour through the tin sifter, the powdery white smoofs hanging in the air covering more of me than the bowl it was meant for. My mess became her miracle as she magically transformed flour and butter and sugar and what-all into sweet rolls that melted in the mouth. Her rolls could not be duplicated by store-bought—it had something to do with a charmed life well-lived and fingers fleshed by the touch of fairy dust.

Soon, Mom, Dad, and my little brother, Charlie, were awakened by the wafting cinnamon scent of sweet rolls. The sun had barely peaked through the kitchen window; Grandma believed the best of life began with a rising sun. Then she would wistfully credit me with the specialness of that day's pastries before we gave thanks and feasted.

These special times with Grandma continued until her death, making my brother and sisters, not to mention aunts and uncles—her children—wonder about the strange bond we shared. I looked forward to the times when we would get together during Thanksgiving or Spring Break, even after I was married and Dustin and Tara were born. We had a connection that transcended the generations between us and formed the core of who I am. Grandma Younkin and me, discussing *Oliver Twist* or Browning's "Rabbi Ben Ezra," rocking once again in the chairs on her porch and eventually at the rest home. *Creak-uch, creak-uch, creak-uch.*

She died at the age of ninety-five, contented, courageous, and serene. I still see her from time to time—the most beautiful person I've ever known, ensconced like royalty in her rocking chair. Nothing else since then has provided such meaning or made me so confident in my worth.

In pensive, troubled moments, wishing I could talk with Grandma, I can still hear the *creak-uch, creak-uch, creak-uch* coming from somewhere familiar and safe. Grandma Younkin whispers, "Remember Marley, Mercutio, Horatio, Puck—remember who you are."

Epilogue

Whistling wind wrestles the four harmonic chimes hanging under the eaves of our back porch deck, the three-tubed bass chimes gonging the main beat for the syncopated *doo-wop* of the multi-tubed tenors and altos which blend uniformly with the robins' trills, the squirrels' chitters, and Oliver's and Twist's (our cats) meows. My mind rests, satisfied and energized by the call to worship in our backyard. Another early morning beckons in Kansas' oldest city nestled next to the Missouri River. I'm reminded, as I sit on the porch's lone rocking chair, of a Mary Oliver line of poetry, "Sometimes I need only to stand wherever I am to be blessed."

Dustin, Tara, and Olivia grew up, in spite of my tribulations, into the savvy adults their tender years forecast: Dustin, principled fighter for the underdog; Tara, gritty, determined champion of holy causes; and, Olivia, empathetic standard bearer for everyone. I wonder how their personalities and relationships would have been altered by older brother, Jordan.

Three grandchildren from Tara and Trent add to our close-knit family: Hunter, Wyatt, and Avery (like Tara, sure to be the drill sergeant of the family). They'll be over to our house later in the morning to play in our backyard—otherwise known as *Grandkids' Heaven*, complete with a sixty-foot zip line, an electric John Deere Jeep, swings, lookouts, and slides. Giggles, shouts, and screams will contrast with nature's stirring sounds, creating an unconventional symphony unmatched by Bach or Mozart. One day, Dustin's and Sarah's baby will join them.

"Jordan is dead, and I'm—I'm responsible." Seven words stimulated by the accusing finger of conscience uttered helplessly to my wife, and then crudely wrapped in guilt and buried deep in my soul for nearly twenty years. It festered into chronic depression I couldn't identify until Palm Sunday of 1994.

I'm still haunted by the opaque tube coming from Jordan's newborn mouth, the rasping breath finally quieted by my decision—the older brother Dustin, Tara, and Olivia would never know. Jordan is watching and waiting for the day when he will embrace each of us.

Stirring at 4:00 A.M. each weekday morning, I awaken without an alarm clock to begin my day: mile-and-a-half walk, brief poetry reading to refresh and focus my mind, cook sausage and egg scramble for Connie and me, and then commute to Blue Valley West High School, forty-five miles away. The teachers at West say I wake up earlier than everyone but God. After school, I'll meet former students like Alexis or Stuart or Frankie at the Black Dog Coffeehouse to talk about their hopes and dreams since graduating from high school.

I agree with Grandma's insistence that literature matters in day-to-day life, that a better existence can be unveiled in the pages of books. I'm now compelled to pass that counsel on to others. I sit in a Queen Anne's chair in our living room on Saturday mornings sipping hot Kona coffee with Morrison, Burke, McCarthy, Angelou, Oliver, and Conroy, knowing that the spirit from their pages connects with mine each time I read them. And so too with my students.

Grandma knew, oh so well.

Nannie Sylvie (Wilson) Younkin graduation from Central Normal College (KS) 1907 as a teacher.

Hiram and Patricia (Younkin) Baxter marriage on January 25, 1947.

Jeffrey Lynn and Charlie outside 1301 Morton house in 1954.

The four Baxter children 1963: Lori (4), Nancy (7), Charlie (11), and Jeffrey Lynn (15).

Connie's and Jeff's three children: Tara (6), Olivia (2), and Dustin (9).

Jeffrey Lynn Great Bend High School graduation 1966.

Connie as Laurey in Oklahoma at the University of Kansas in 1972.

Jeff and Connie preparing to leave for the Institute of Peace in Washington, D.C. to celebrate at a banquet for the National State Teachers of the Year in May 2014.